G R A D E

02
KEYBOARDS

Published by
Trinity College London Press Ltd
trinitycollege.com

Registered in England
Company no. 09726123

Photography by Zute Lightfoot, lightfootphoto.com

© Copyright 2017 Trinity College London Press Ltd
Third impression, March 2020

Printed in England by Caligraving Ltd

Parental and Teacher Guidance:

The songs in Trinity's Rock & Pop syllabus have been arranged
to represent the artists' original recordings as closely and
authentically as possible. Popular music frequently deals with
subject matter that some may find offensive or challenging.
It is possible that the songs may include material that some
might find unsuitable for use with younger learners.

We recommend that parents and teachers exercise their own
judgement to satisfy themselves that the lyrics of selected
songs are appropriate for the students concerned. As you
will be aware, there is no requirement that all songs in this
syllabus must be learned. Trinity does not associate itself with,
adopt or endorse any of the opinions or views expressed in
the selected songs.

THE EXAM AT A GLANCE

In your exam you will perform a set of three songs and one of the session skills assessments. You can choose the order of your set list.

SONG 1

Choose a song from this book.

SONG 2

Choose *either* a different song from this book
or a song from the list of additional Trinity Rock & Pop arrangements, available at trinityrock.com
or a song you have chosen yourself: this could be your own cover version or a song that you have written. It should be at the same level as the songs in this book and match the parameters at trinityrock.com

SONG 3: TECHNICAL FOCUS

Song 3 is designed to help you develop specific and relevant techniques in performance. Choose one of the technical focus songs from this book, which cover two specific technical elements.

SESSION SKILLS

Choose *either* **playback** *or* **improvising**.

Session skills are an essential part of every Rock & Pop exam. They are designed to help you develop the techniques music industry performers need.

Sample tests are available in our *Session Skills* books and free examples can be downloaded from trinityrock.com

ACCESS ALL AREAS

GET THE FULL ROCK & POP EXPERIENCE ONLINE AT TRINITYROCK.COM

We have created a range of digital resources to support your learning and give you insider information from the music industry, available online. You will find support, advice and digital content on:

- Songs, performance and technique
- Session skills
- The music industry

You can access tips and tricks from industry professionals featuring:

- Bite-sized videos that include tips from professional musicians on techniques used in the songs
- 'Producer's notes' on the tracks, to increase your knowledge of rock and pop
- Blog posts on performance tips, musical styles, developing technique and advice from the music industry

JOIN US ONLINE AT:

 /TRINITYROCKANDPOP    @TRINITY_ROCK    /TRINITYROCKANDPOP   and at TRINITYROCK.COM

CONTENTS

BORN TO BE WILD	5	TECHNICAL FOCUS
IN MY PLACE	10	
CHANDELIER	15	TECHNICAL FOCUS
MISS YOU	23	
JUST KISSED MY BABY	27	TECHNICAL FOCUS
SEASONS (WAITING ON YOU)	33	
UPTOWN FUNK	38	
VIDEO GAMES	44	
HELP PAGES	48	

THE AUDIO

Professional demo & backing tracks can be downloaded free, see inside cover for details.

Music preparation and book layout by Andrew Skirrow for Camden Music Services
Music consultants: Nick Crispin, Chris Walters, Christopher Hussey, Julie Parker
Drums recorded by Cab Grant and Jake Watson at AllStar Studios, Chelmsford
All other audio arranged, recorded & produced by Tom Fleming
Keys arrangements: Nigel Fletcher, Simon Foxley, Christopher Hussey & Mal Maddock

Musicians
Keys, Bass & Guitar: Tom Fleming
Drums: George Double
Vocals: Bo Walton, Brendan Reilly, Hayley Sanderson, Tom Adamson

YOUR
PAGE
NOTES

TECHNICAL FOCUS

BORN TO BE WILD
STEPPENWOLF

WORDS AND MUSIC: MARS BONFIRE

02 GRADE
KEYBOARDS

SINGLE BY
Steppenwolf

ALBUM
Steppenwolf

B-SIDE
Everybody's Next One

RELEASED
29 January 1968 (album)

RECORDED
**Autumn 1967
American Recording
Co. Studio, Los Angeles
California, USA**

LABEL
**Dunhill
RCA**

WRITER
Mars Bonfire

PRODUCER
Gabriel Mekler

Although based in southern California, Steppenwolf evolved out of a Canadian band, The Sparrow. The line-up for Steppenwolf's first two albums was John Kay (vocals, guitar), Michael Monarch (guitar), Rushton Moreve (bass), Goldy McJohn (keyboards) and Jerry Edmonton (drums). The band's first six albums made the US top 20, and six of their singles were top-40 hits.

'Born to be Wild' was written by Jerry Edmonton's guitarist brother and former Sparrow bandmate Dennis under his stage name Mars Bonfire. The song featured on Steppenwolf's self-titled 1968 debut album and was released as its third single. It was the band's breakthrough hit, reaching No. 2 in the US for three consecutive weeks, kept from the top only by The Rascals' 'People Got to be Free'. The following year the song was used in its entirety in Dennis Hopper's directorial film debut *Easy Rider*, the biker road trip counterculture classic also starring Peter Fonda and Jack Nicholson. (Another Steppenwolf song, 'The Pusher', was also used in the film.) The song includes the lyric 'heavy metal thunder' and is credited for introducing the phrase 'heavy metal' into popular culture, which soon became a commonly used term for a louder, more aggressive style of hard rock.

TECHNICAL FOCUS

The following technical focus elements are featured in this song:

- Coordination
- Solo

This song features a driving bass line that will require careful **coordination** with the right-hand chords (bar 5 onwards). Later, the extended **solo** will test your familiarity with the E blues scale. You'll need to play with soloistic abandon while maintaining a solid left-hand groove and playing the semiquavers in bars 38 and 44 with precision. Look out for the held E in bar 39. The suggested sound for this song is organ, if available.

BORN TO BE WILD

WORDS AND MUSIC: MARS BONFIRE

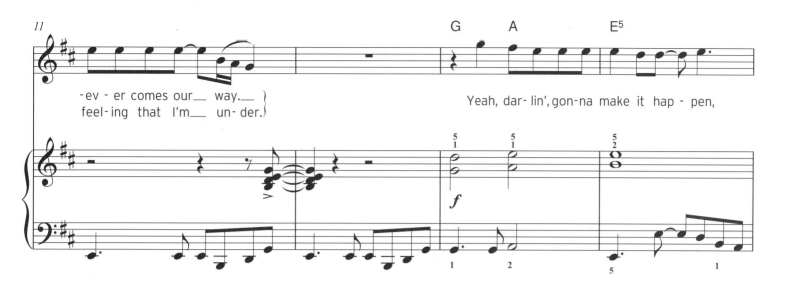

-ev - er comes our__ way.__ }
feel-ing that I'm__ un-der.)

Yeah, dar-lin', gon-na make it hap - pen,

take the world in a love em-brace.__

Fire all of your guns__ at once__ and

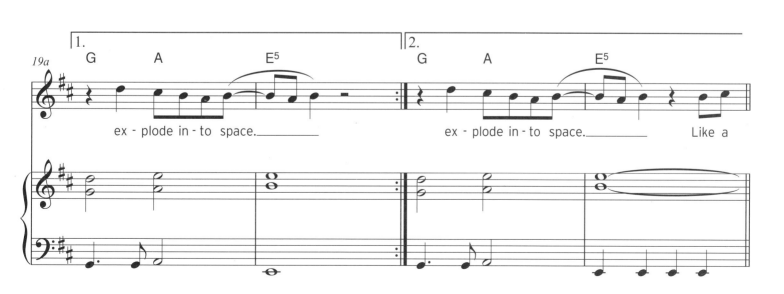

ex - plode in - to space.__

ex - plode in - to space.__ Like a

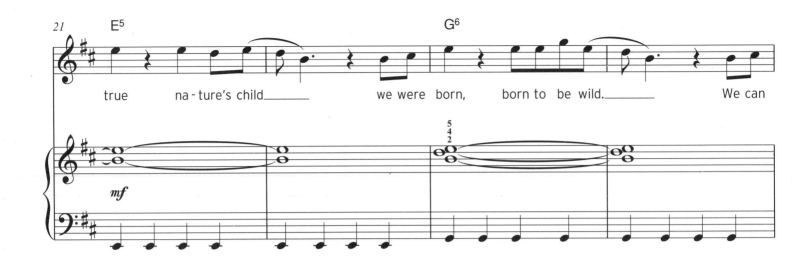

true na-ture's child_____ we were born, born to be wild._____ We can

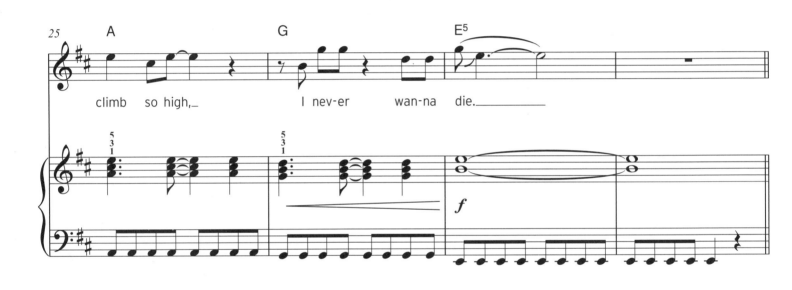

climb so high,__ I nev-er wan-na die._____

Born to be wild,_____

born   to   be   wild._____

Solo

SINGLE BY
Coldplay

ALBUM
A Rush of Blood to the Head

B-SIDE
One I Love
I Bloom Blaum

RELEASED
5 August 2002

RECORDED
September 2001–May 2002 (album)

LABEL
Parlophone

WRITERS
Chris Martin
Jonny Buckland
Guy Berryman
Will Champion

PRODUCERS
Ken Nelson
Coldplay

IN MY PLACE
COLDPLAY

WORDS AND MUSIC: CHRIS MARTIN, JONNY BUCKLAND
GUY BERRYMAN, WILL CHAMPION

After breaking through in 2000 with the single 'Yellow', Coldplay quickly became one of the biggest bands of the new millennium. Their melodic mix of introspective ballads and anthemic rock has earned the British quartet sales in the millions, as well as worldwide popularity and numerous awards.

'In My Place' was the first single to be released from Coldplay's second album, 2002's *A Rush of Blood to the Head*, preceding the album by three weeks. It peaked at No. 2 in the UK singles chart and helped propel the album to No. 1 in the UK, Europe and Australia. 'In My Place' was the first song recorded for the album and chosen as its lead single 'because it was the song that made us want to do a second album. It kept us going and made us think we could still write songs,' according to frontman Chris Martin. The band were performing the song some time before the release of *Rush of Blood to the Head*, including as an encore at their first Glastonbury Festival headline set in June 2002, two months before the album was released.

⚡ PERFORMANCE TIPS

This song is an accompaniment arrangement of a guitar-led song. This means that you play some lines that are played by the guitar in the original version, for example the opening riff in the right hand, which should be played with a strong, ringing sound. Take care to drop down to *mp* in bar 7 when the vocal comes in and observe the other dynamic contrasts throughout the song. Also look out for occasional rhythmic complexity in the left hand. Piano is a suitable sound here.

IN MY PLACE

WORDS AND MUSIC:

CHRIS MARTIN, JONNY BUCKLAND
GUY BERRYMAN, WILL CHAMPION

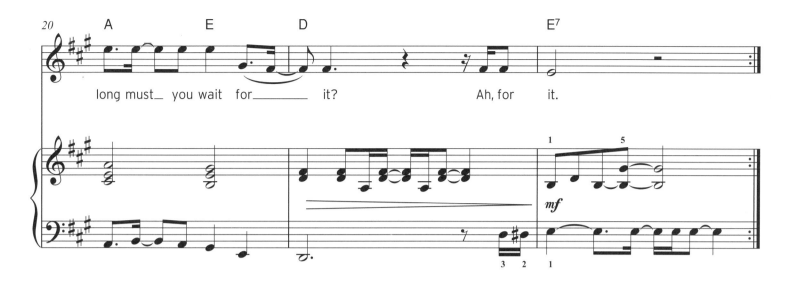

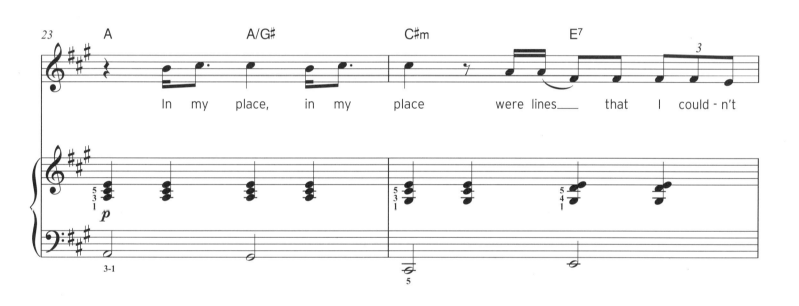

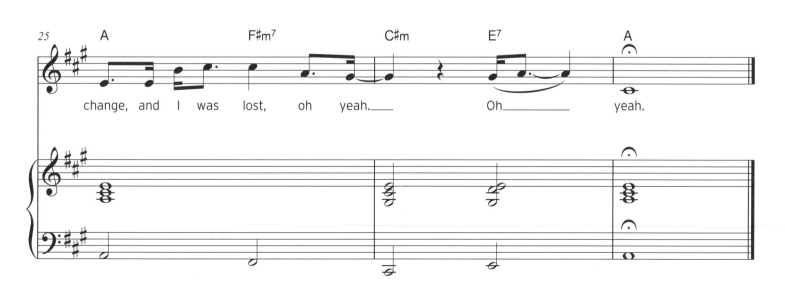

YOUR
PAGE
NOTES

TECHNICAL FOCUS

CHANDELIER
SIA

WORDS AND MUSIC: SIA FURLER, JESSE SHATKIN

SINGLE BY
Sia

ALBUM
1000 Forms of Fear

RELEASED
17 March 2014

RECORDED
2013

LABEL
**Inertia
Monkey Puzzle
RCA**

WRITERS
**Sia Furler
Jesse Shatkin**

PRODUCERS
**Greg Kurstin
Jesse Shatkin**

Singer and songwriter Sia Furler is from Adelaide, Australia, and first gained attention for her vocals on Zero 7's 2001 debut album. She scored huge international success across a succession of solo albums as well as co-writing hits for numerous artists, including Beyoncé, Britney Spears, Rihanna, Shakira, Christina Aguilera, Celine Dion, Rita Ora, Ne-Yo, Flo Rida and David Guetta.

'Chandelier' is the song that brought the spotlight-shunning Sia to international stardom. The lead single from her sixth studio album, 2014's *1000 Forms of Fear*, the song became a top-ten hit in over 25 countries with sales in excess of three million in the US alone. The accompanying video has become one of the top 20 most viewed YouTube videos ever with 1.4 billion views, which helped secure Sia's first No. 1 album in both her native Australia and the US. The song stemmed from an impromptu jam session between Sia and producer Jesse Shatkin, with Sia playing piano and Shatkin the marimba, and came together in minutes, according to the singer. *Billboard* magazine voted 'Chandelier' the best song of 2014, stating that 'few could have seen 'Chandelier' coming, and an unforeseen triumph like this one helps make pop music so exciting as an art form.'

TECHNICAL FOCUS

The following two technical focus elements are featured in this song:

- Arpeggiated chords
- Octave leaps

At bars 17–22 you'll need to keep the driving groove going while ensuring that the two-note **arpeggiated chords** are exactly together and coordinated with the left hand. From bar 25 to bar 70, the left-hand bass line is reliant on **octave leaps** in an increasingly complex rhythmic pattern. Aim for precision and a strong, consistent sound. If available, electric piano and synth would both work well as sounds for this song.

TECHNICAL FOCUS
CHANDELIER

WORDS AND MUSIC:
SIA FURLER, JESSE SHATKIN

RnB ♩ = **87** (1½ bars count-in)

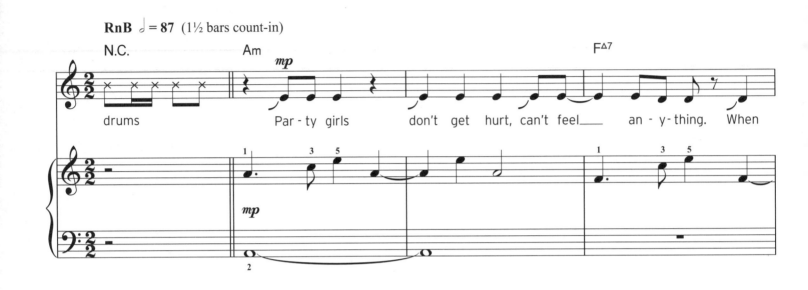

drums Par-ty girls don't get hurt, can't feel___ an-y-thing. When

will I learn?___ I push it down,___ I push it dow - ow-own.___

I'm the one for a 'good-time' call; phone's blow-ing up,___ they're ring-ing my door-bell. I

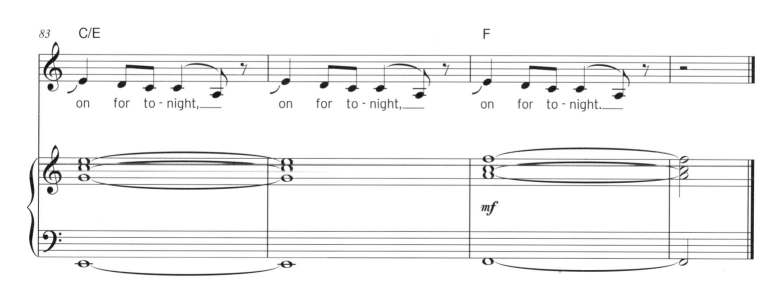

YOUR
PAGE
NOTES

SINGLE BY
The Rolling Stones

ALBUM
Some Girls

B-SIDE
Far Away Eyes

RELEASED
10 May 1978

RECORDED
10 October–21 December 1977, Pathé Marconi Studios, Paris, France

WRITERS
**Mick Jagger
Keith Richards**

PRODUCERS
The Glimmer Twins

MISS YOU
THE ROLLING STONES

WORDS AND MUSIC: MICK JAGGER, KEITH RICHARDS

The Rolling Stones rivalled The Beatles as the biggest band of the 1960s, but unlike the latter endured into the 1970s and beyond. Led by Mick Jagger on vocals and Keith Richards on guitar with Charlie Watts on drums, their line-up has also included Bill Wyman on bass (1962-1993) and Ronnie Wood on guitar (1975 to the present day).

'Miss You' was written by Jagger with Billy Preston, a keyboard player who guested on The Beatles' final two albums and went on to record and tour with the Stones from 1971 until 1977. 'Billy had shown me the four-on-the-floor bass drum part, and I would just play the guitar,' said Jagger. Preston also came up with the song's disco-indebted bass line, with a little 'changing and polishing, but the basic idea was Billy's,' according to Wyman. Additional musicians on the track included harmonica player Sugar Blue, who was found busking in Paris where the song was recorded, King Crimson's Mel Collins on sax and Small Faces keyboard player Ian MacLagan on electric piano. The song reached No. 3 in the UK and became the band's eighth and final US chart topper.

⚡ PERFORMANCE TIPS

This song was inspired by the disco movement, so it needs to be played with a cool sense of groove. There are frequent 'fills' between the sung passages – you may wish to practise the A minor pentatonic and A blues scales to help familiarise yourself with the notes needed for these. You might like to use an electric piano sound if this is available (a Wurlitzer was used on the original recording), and pay attention to the detailed articulation markings which appear throughout the song.

MISS YOU

WORDS AND MUSIC:
MICK JAGGER, KEITH RICHARDS

Rock ♩ = 106 (2 bars count-in)

1. I been hold-ing out__ so long,__ I been sleep-in' all__ a-lone;__ Lord, I miss you.

(2.) haunt-ed in__ my sleep,__ you been star-ring in__ my dreams;__ Lord, I miss you,

I been hang-in' on__ the phone,__ I been sleep-in' all__ a-lone;__ I wan-na

I been wait-in' in__ the hall,__ I been wait'-in on__ your call;__ Lord, I

TECHNICAL FOCUS

JUST KISSED MY BABY

THE METERS

**WORDS AND MUSIC: ZIGGY MODELISTE, ART NEVILLE
LEO NOCENTELLI, GEORGE PORTER JR.**

SONG BY
The Meters

ALBUM
Rejuvenation

RELEASED
July 1974 (album)

LABEL
Reprise

WRITERS
**Ziggy Modeliste
Art Neville
Leo Nocentelli
George Porter Jr.**

PRODUCERS
**Allen Toussaint
The Meters**

The Meters were a New Orleans funk band formed in 1965 by keys player Art Neville (of the Neville Brothers), guitarist Leo Nocentelli, drummer Joseph 'Zigaboo' Modeliste and bassist George Porter Jr. From the late 60s to late 70s they played on most of the city's R&B hits as house band for the legendary Allen Toussaint, as well as scoring several US hits in their own right.

The Meters' syncopated revamping of New Orleans rhythm and blues has proved to be hugely influential on popular music. Playing on (and in many cases co-writing) hit records for Toussaint-produced artists such as Lee Dorsey, Irma Thomas and Dr John helped earn them a reputation as the city's equivalent of Detroit's Funk Brothers or Memphis's Booker T & the MG's, house bands for the Motown and Stax labels respectively. 'Just Kissed My Baby' is from The Meters' fifth album, *Rejuvenation*, released in 1974. That same year the band also backed Labelle on their US No. 1 hit 'Lady Marmalade' and Robert Palmer on his debut album *Sneakin' Sally Through the Alley*.

TECHNICAL FOCUS

The following two technical focus elements are featured in this song:

- Offbeat quavers
- Staccato and accent markings

As with all funk, rhythm and groove are highly important in this song. The **offbeat quavers** offer a rhythmic challenge throughout, and you'll need to play these accurately and without speeding up. The **staccato and accent markings** are important in this genre, so take care to observe these, for example in bars 6 and 7 (and similarly for the rest of the song). Use an organ sound if this is available on your instrument.

JUST KISSED MY BABY

WORDS AND MUSIC:
ZIGGY MODELISTE, ART NEVILLE
LEO NOCENTELLI, GEORGE PORTER JR.

Funk ♩ = **84** (2 bars count-in)

N.C.

(guitar riff)   *mf*

% G7(♯9)

1. I feel   like a king,   yeah,___   'cause I just___
4. I feel   so good in-side,   'cause I just___

1st time: *mf*
2nd time: *f*

To Coda ⊕

YOUR
PAGE
NOTES

SEASONS (WAITING ON YOU) FUTURE ISLANDS

WORDS AND MUSIC: WILLIAM CASHION, SAMUEL T. HERRING GERRIT WELMERS

SINGLE BY
Future Islands

ALBUM
Singles

B-SIDE
One Day

RELEASED
4 February 2014

RECORDED
**August 2013
Dreamland Studios
Hurley, New York, USA**

LABEL
4AD

WRITERS
**William Cashion
Samuel T. Herring
Gerrit Welmers**

PRODUCER
Chris Coady

The three members of Future Islands met at university in North Carolina and released their debut album in 2006. Featuring Samuel T Herring (vocals), Gerrit Welmers (keyboards/programming) and William Cashion (bass/guitars), the band found international success with the release of their fourth album, 2014's *Singles*.

Before the release of 'Seasons (Waiting on You)', Future Islands were a little-known, cult act. The event that really changed the band's fortunes overnight occurred on 3 March 2014, when they made their network television debut on *The Late Show with David Letterman*, performing the song live. Herring's intense delivery and show-stealing moves elicited an effusive reaction from the host and viewing audience, before becoming a viral hit around the world after the clip was posted on YouTube. Eight years after forming, the band found themselves to be overnight sensations, suddenly being offered high-profile TV spots and festival slots around the world. By the end of 2014, 'Seasons' had been voted the top song of the year by *NME*, *Spin*, *The Village Voice*, *Time Out*, *Pitchfork* and *Consequence of Sound*.

⚡ PERFORMANCE TIPS

This song is firmly rooted in the synth-pop genre and, while it can be played on piano, it's much more effective on a keyboard with a good synth sound (try to find a sound that's as close as possible to the one used in the original version). Count the left-hand rhythm carefully in bars 1 and 5, and make sure that you pick up the groove at the right tempo in bar 9. Take care where notes are tied over into the next chord, for example at bars 34, 36 and elsewhere.

SEASONS (WAITING ON YOU)

WORDS AND MUSIC:

WILLIAM CASHION, SAMUEL T. HERRING, GERRIT WELMERS

Synthpop ♩ = 70 (2 bars count-in)

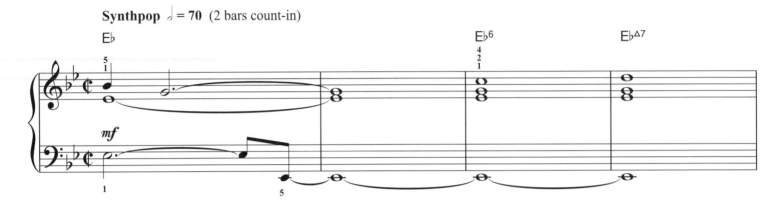

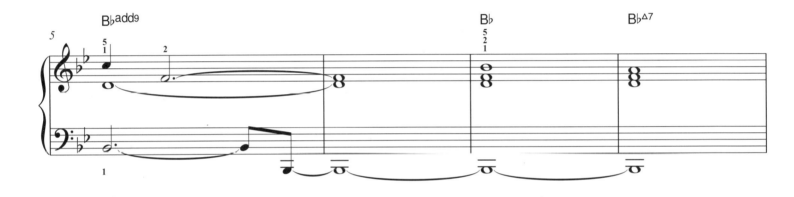

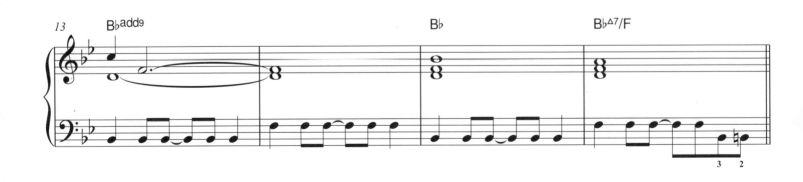

will crave_____ what is gone,____ will crave

what is gone,_____ gone a - way.____

'Cause I've been wait - ing on you.____

SINGLE BY
**Mark Ronson
feat. Bruno Mars**

ALBUM
Uptown Special

RELEASED
10 November 2014

RECORDED
**2014, Royal Studios
Memphis, Tennessee, USA**

**Zelig Studios
London, England**

**Cherry Beach Studios
Toronto, Ontario, Canada**

**The Armory, Vancouver
British Columbia, Canada**

**Levcon Studios, Los
Angeles, California, USA**

**Daptone Studios, New
York City, New York, USA**

LABEL
RCA

WRITERS
**Mark Ronson, Jeff Bhasker
Bruno Mars etc. (see left)**

PRODUCERS
**Mark Ronson, Jeff Bhasker
Bruno Mars**

UPTOWN FUNK
MARK RONSON
FEAT. BRUNO MARS

WORDS AND MUSIC: MARK RONSON, JEFF BHASKER, BRUNO MARS
PHILIP LAWRENCE, NICHOLAS WILLIAMS
DEVON GALLASPY, LONNIE SIMMONS
RONNIE WILSON, CHARLES WILSON
ROBERT WILSON, RUDOLPH TAYLOR

Mark Ronson is an English musician, producer, songwriter and DJ schooled in hip-hop, R&B, funk, soul, pop and rock. He came to prominence in the 2000s with his productions for the likes of Lily Allen, Christina Aguilera and Amy Winehouse alongside his own highly collaborative solo output.

This exuberant homage to the 1980s electro-funk sound of Prince and The Time was written and produced by Ronson with Jeff Bhasker and Bruno Mars, who provides the lead vocal as well as playing drums on the track. It follows the success of the trio's previous collaboration on Mars's 2012 'Locked Out of Heaven', which reached No. 1 in the US. The song took over a half a year to complete, with 82 takes on the guitar part alone. It became the best-selling single of 2015 on both sides of the Atlantic, topping the charts for 14 consecutive weeks in the US and a total of seven weeks in the UK. It won three Grammy Awards, including the prestigious Record of the Year, as well as the Brit Award for British Single of the Year. The video received its billionth view on YouTube in September 2015, becoming YouTube's third most watched video in history.

⚡ PERFORMANCE TIPS

As with all funk, rhythmic precision is vital in this song, so practise the dotted quaver/semiquaver rhythm carefully. Count the long rests near the start carefully, and make sure that you don't speed up on the rising offbeat notes in bars 25-27. Electric piano is the suggested sound, but you could use other sounds too, for example a synth sound for the chords in bars 29-36. If you have a bass sound similar to the one on the original track, it could be fun to use that as well.

UPTOWN FUNK

WORDS AND MUSIC: MARK RONSON, JEFF BHASKER, BRUNO MARS
PHILIP LAWRENCE NICHOLAS WILLIAMS, DEVON GALLASPY
LONNIE SIMMONS, RONNIE WILSON, CHARLES WILSON
ROBERT WILSON, RUDOLPH TAYLOR

up - town funk gon' give it to you. 'Cause up - town funk gon' give it to you.

Sat - ur - day night__ and we in the spot.__ Don't be - lieve__ me? Just watch.

Don't be - lieve__ me? Just watch.

Don't be - lieve__ me? Just watch.

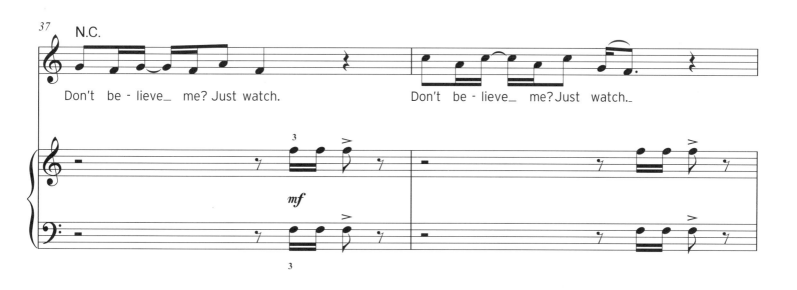

Don't be - lieve__ me? Just watch.

Don't be - lieve__ me? Just watch.__

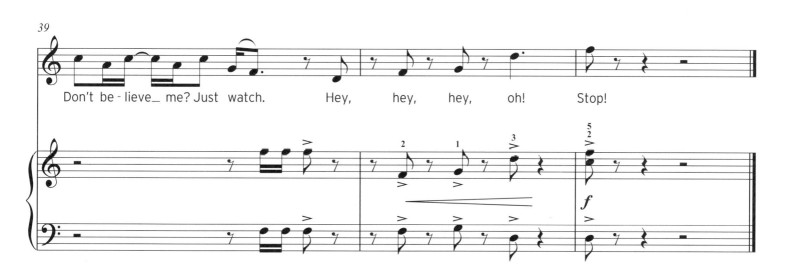

Don't be - lieve__ me? Just watch. Hey, hey, hey, oh! Stop!

SINGLE BY
Lana Del Rey

ALBUM
Born to Die

B-SIDE
Blue Jeans

RELEASED
7 October 2011

RECORDED
2011
BMG Studios, New York City, New York, USA

LABEL
Stranger Records
Interscope
Polydor

WRITERS
Lana Del Rey
Justin Parker

PRODUCER
Robopop

VIDEO GAMES
LANA DEL REY

WORDS AND MUSIC: LANA DEL REY, JUSTIN PARKER

Please note: This song contains subject matter that some might find inappropriate for younger learners. Please refer to the Parental and Teacher Guidance at the beginning of this book for more information.

Born Elizabeth Grant, Lana Del Rey is a singer and songwriter from New York who found international fame with her second album, 2012's *Born to Die*, which topped the charts in ten countries including the UK. It was the year's fifth best-selling album worldwide with sales of over 3.4 million copies.

'Video Games' was first released to the internet on 29 June 2011, accompanied by a video Del Rey made herself using a webcam and footage taken from YouTube. It became a viral sensation and subsequently viewed more than 127 million times, leading to her signing a major label deal for her album, *Born to Die*. Del Rey co-wrote the song with English composer Justin Parker, who collaborated on five of the album's songs including the title track, released as its second single. 'Video Games' was a big international hit, reaching the top ten in 14 countries. It earned Del Rey an Ivor Novello Award for Best Contemporary Song, while NME named it Best Track of the Year. The romantic melancholia encapsulated in the song led Del Rey to comment: 'It's just really sad, it's myself in song form.'

⚡ PERFORMANCE TIPS

This solo piano arrangement will require you to play the right-hand melody smoothly and with expression. Try to make an even sound on the repeated semiquavers, which should all be the same volume. It may help to practise moving around in fifths in your left hand. Look out for frequent changes of left-hand clef. Piano is the recommended sound for this song, as used in the original version.

VIDEO GAMES

WORDS AND MUSIC:
LANA DEL REY, JUSTIN PARKER

Ballad ♩ = 62 (2 bars count-in)

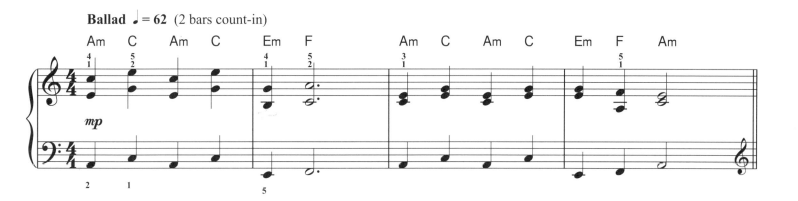

Swing-ing in the back-yard, pull up in your fast car, whis-tl-ing my name.

O-pen up a beer, and you say, "Get o-ver here and play a vid-e-o game." I'm

in his fav-'rite sun dress, watch-ing me get un-dressed, take that bo-dy down-town.

CHOOSING SONGS FOR YOUR EXAM

SONG 1

Choose a song from this book.

SONG 2

Choose a song which is:

Either a different song from this book

or from the list of additional Trinity Rock & Pop arrangements, available at trinityrock.com

or from a printed or online source

or your own arrangement

or a song that you have written yourself

You can play Song 2 unaccompanied or with a backing track (minus the keyboard part). If you like, you can create a backing track yourself (or with friends), add your own vocals, or be accompanied live by another musician.

The level of difficulty and length of the song should be similar to the songs in this book and match the parameters available at trinityrock.com

When choosing a song, think about:

- Does it work on my instrument?

- Are there any technical elements that are too difficult for me? (If so, perhaps save it for when you do the next grade)

- Do I enjoy playing it?

- Does it work with my other songs to create a good set list?

SONG 3: TECHNICAL FOCUS

Song 3 is designed to help you develop specific and relevant techniques in performance. Choose one of the technical focus songs from this book, which cover two specific technical elements.

SHEET MUSIC

If your choice for Song 2 is not from this book, you must provide the examiner with a photocopy. The title, writers of the song and your name should be on the sheet music. You must also bring an original copy of the book, or a download version with proof of purchase, for each song that you perform in the exam.

Your music can be:

- A lead sheet with lyrics, chords and melody line

- A chord chart with lyrics

- A full score using conventional staff notation

PLAYING WITH BACKING TRACKS

All your backing tracks can be downloaded from soundwise.co.uk

- The backing tracks begin with a click track, which sets the tempo and helps you start accurately

- Be careful to balance the volume of the backing track against your instrument

- Listen carefully to the backing track to ensure that you are playing in time

- Keyboard players should not use auto-accompaniment features for these exams as the aim is to play with a backing track

If you are creating your own backing track, here are some further tips:

- Make sure that the sound quality is of a good standard

- Think carefully about the instruments/sounds you are using on the backing track

- Avoid copying what you are playing in the exam on the backing track – it should support, not duplicate

- Do you need to include a click track at the beginning?

COPYRIGHT IN A SONG

If you are a singer, instrumentalist or songwriter it is important to know about copyright. When someone writes a song they automatically own the copyright (sometimes called 'the rights'). Copyright begins once a piece of music has been documented or recorded (eg by video, CD or score notation) and protects the interests of the creators. This means that others cannot copy it, sell it, make it available online or record it without the owner's permission or the appropriate licence.

COVER VERSIONS

- When an artist creates a new version of a song it is called a 'cover version'

- The majority of songwriters subscribe to licensing agencies, also known as 'collecting societies'. When a songwriter is a member of such an agency, the performing rights to their material are transferred to the agency (this includes cover versions of their songs)

- The agency works on the writer's behalf by issuing licences to performance venues, who report what songs have been played, which in turn means that the songwriter will receive a payment for any songs used

- You can create a cover version of a song and use it in an exam without needing a licence

There are different rules for broadcasting (eg TV, radio, internet), selling or copying (pressing CDs, DVDs etc), and for printed material, and the appropriate licences should be sought out.

YOUR
PAGE
NOTES

YOUR
PAGE
NOTES

YOUR
PAGE
NOTES